NE

BLU^{THE}**E**BIRDS **2**

G000144592

NEVER MIND
BLU*THE*EBIRDS 2

Another Ultimate
CARDIFF
CITY
QUIZ BOOK

DAVID COLLINS
& GARETH BENNETT

The
History
Press

Dedicated to Cardiff City fans everywhere.
If it matters to you, like it matters to us,
then this book is for you.

First published 2013

The History Press
The Mill, Brimscombe Port
Stroud, Gloucestershire, GL5 2QG
www.thehistorypress.co.uk

© David Collins & Gareth Bennett, 2013

The right of David Collins & Gareth Bennett to be identified
as the Authors of this work has been asserted in accordance with
the Copyrights, Designs and Patents Act 1988.

All rights reserved. No part of this book may be reprinted
or reproduced or utilised in any form or by any electronic,
mechanical or other means, now known or hereafter invented,
including photocopying and recording, or in any information
storage or retrieval system, without the permission in writing
from the Publishers.

British Library Cataloguing in Publication Data.
A catalogue record for this book is available from the British Library.

ISBN 978 0 7524 9780 8

Typesetting and origination by The History Press
Printed in Great Britain

Contents

Foreword

I am delighted to once again recommend this marvellous quiz book to you. I am sure that, like me, you will enjoy pondering the many questions as the boys take you on another journey back through the mists of time.

This book is so much more than just dull questions and answers. it's a joke book, history book, almanac and biography. David & Gareth's unique style has helped them display their own personality whilst still producing a book which will appeal to City fans of all ages.

Once again, there are questions on players, terrace songs, games and goals, following the successful format of their first quiz book (still available at all good book shops of course!)

Having been proud to pull on the Cardiff City colours on many occasions myself, the book brought back so many happy (and some less happy!) memories of lads like Tony Evans, Clive Charles and dear old Jimmy Andrews. Plus of course, who can forget that man Robin Friday! So many memories brought to life in these pages.

I am sure that you will enjoy this book once again. David & Gareth have hit on a unique idea here and I look forward to following their writing career closely over the coming years.

David Giles, 12 Welsh Caps
Cardiff City 1974–1978 and 1985–1987

Introduction

We are back.

Tempted once more to commit our thoughts to print in the name of posterity.

We were simply unable to resist the challenge of producing another quiz book based upon the glorious history, achievements and contribution to society that is ... Cardiff City Football Club.

'Tis true. We could not hide from the chance to wade back through history, to play a part in the literary heritage of our glorious club and, humbly & modestly, take our own places in football folklore.

Plus the publishers made us a really good offer.

The format of this book is simple enough. We ask the questions and you shout out the answers. Rocket science it is not.

This book fits easily into a glove compartment or rucksack. Take it away with you as you set off for Spurs and Arsenal. The easy questions will get you to Chelsea, Swansea, and West Bromwich Albion, while the harder rounds might last you as far as Manchester, Liverpool and beyond. We also find it works well at home games as an alternative to talking to our mates in the pub. Never did care for all that socialising stuff.

All the answers are right. They just are. We know our stuff. So don't write in if you think we won the FA Cup in 1827 or Benny Miller played up front in the Carling Cup Final. It just didn't happen, OK?

We have also had regard to the availability of modern technology as a research tool. So while, if you really wanted, you could surf the internet for details of players, goals and games, we have also included a great number of questions which, to be honest, you would have to have been there to know the answer. And we are guessing that, many, many times ... like us, you were indeed there.

Once again, we have included as much up-to-date information as possible to support the historical bits. We left it as late as possible before introducing a cut-off point around September 2013. Not quite time to include any questions about our signing of Lionel Messi in time for games over Christmas, sorry. Never mind; maybe we'll pick up on that in 'Never Mind the Bluebirds 3'.

David Collins & Gareth Bennett

The 'Current Affairs' Round

Welcome to our book.

We hope you enjoy this second season syndrome stroll through the history of our football club, uncovering stones along the way, with trips and stumbles over how much you really know about Cardiff City Football Club.

We go from Riverside AFC, through the heady 1920s into great days on the infamous Grange End, Eddie May's Barmy Army and today's burning issues of Red versus Blue and the intricacies of the Malaysian Stock Exchange. All of football life is here.

But to kick off, a straightforward round, all about last season. Another lacklustre showing; a dull, uneventful season where we trundled along in mid-table and life went sleepily on.

Yeah, like that's ever gonna happen …

Get stuck into these then. To start with, a few about season 2012/13 – did you blink and miss it? Shame on you …

1   Towards the end of that season of seasons, City signed defender Leon Barnett on loan as cover for the injured Mark Hudson. From which club did he come?

2 We are sure that you all remember that historic night last season against Charlton Athletic as, finally, City clinched promotion. But history also played its own part that night. What was significant about the specific date of the game?

3 Who were City's next opponents immediately after that historic night. Another special occasion, we recall.

4 In how many countries can you watch Cardiff City on TV in the Premier League? We will give you five either way!

5 Who scored a last-minute penalty in (hopefully!) City's last-ever Championship game last season?

These next few are about events of the close season. Footballers may have had the summer off, but not us quiz-masters.

6 From which club did the Bluebirds sign 'the Pitbull' this year?

7 Which Cardiff City player played for England against Scotland in August 2013?

8 Who is the current chairman of Cardiff City?

9 What is our shirt sponsorship logo these days?

10 Who said 'when he is hard, Vincent Tan is the ace of diamonds; where he is soft, he is the ace of hearts'?

11 Who captained Cardiff City in the first ever Premier
League game?

The future starts here.

I Write the Songs

If you enjoyed singing along to our round on terrace anthems in our earlier book, then this will also be right up your street – or even on your terrace.

This time though, we are not looking for a player's identity. Instead, we want you to complete the lyrics. Extra points – of course – for singing along (especially if you are reading this on the bus).

(This round might just help you decide if you are up to the intellectual challenge posed by this book or not. It's Karaoke City AFC!)

1   Easy one to start … 'and its Cardiff City. Cardiff City FC …' (so what comes next?)

2   'Ooooooo Ahhhh …'

3   'Ooh Ah …'

4 'Oh – Willie Willie ...'

5 'Oh oh oh oh oh ... Fraizer Campbell will always score goals. Every chance that he gets ...'

6 'Peter Whittingham, he does ...'

7 'He plays on the left, he plays on the right – that boy Chris Burke, makes ... (who?) look shite.'

Altogether now, 'Peter Whittingham ...'

8 'John Buchanan, John Buchanan ...'

9 'Ole, ole, ole, ole ...'

10 'Open the score Richards ...'

11 'We want Sam Hammam ...'

Round 3

View from
the Dug-Out

Ah, the Boss, the Gaffer, the Guv'nor. The hot seat. The managerial merry-go-round!

But how much can you recall about the men at the top? Are you are a new recruit weaned on Malky's fist pump, or do you go back to Eddie May's Army? Who ran the show after the war? And who was 'Archie'?

It's tough at the top, as you will see …

1 Arguably our most famous manager, but tough Scot Jimmy Scoular (1964–1973) managed which other Welsh club?

2 Bobby Gould had a spell in charge at Cardiff City, during what may now seem like very turbulent days indeed. Where did he begin his playing career though? (Clue: he returned there as manager in 1992 after leaving West Bromwich Albion.)

3   Which former Charlton Athletic boss was our manager when Cardiff City beat QPR at the Millennium Stadium Play Off final in 2003?

4   Who was in charge immediately before and after the Second World War?

5   Bobby Gould was succeeded as manager by which other member of the 'Crazy Gang'?

6   Straightforward one now. Who was in charge when Cardiff City won the FA Cup in 1927?

7   Tricky one next – well we had to think about it a bit anyway. Can you tell us who was the last ex-City player to later manage the club?

8   We seemed to go through managers like they were going out of fashion in the late 1990s. During this particularly confusing spell, Terry Yorath was a director and team manager during the 1994/95 season, while Kenny Hibbitt, strangely, had two spells as manager between 1995 and 1998. They also both once played for the same Midlands club – though not at the same time. Can you name that club?

9   Which manager sold John Toshack to Liverpool?

10   Where was Malky Mackay born? Specifically, we
     mean. We won't accept just 'Scotland'. (We only want
     the town, mind; you don't need to go as far as '23
     McGonagall Street'.)

11   Go on then, we know you are dying to tell us. Which City
     boss was referred to as 'Archie' by some of the players,
     especially one R. Friday Esq? (A bit of a clue, perhaps.)

Round

4

Class
Dismissed!

Exciting times, these days, eh? Cardiff City rubbing shoulders with the great and the good.

Football isn't always a constant source of joy, of course. Maybe that's what makes it so appealing. For every glorious goal, there's the odd shameful episode. We opened our 'Big Boy's Book of Bad Boys', and came up with the following – an entire team of banished Bluebirds. Have you got their (red) cards marked?

1 In 1925 at Maine Road, which Scottish international right-back became the first City player to be sent off in a League game?

2 In a 1960 Welsh Cup quarter-final at the Vetch, which two City players were dismissed? (Clue: one was a winger who was a trier, the other a black inside forward.)

3   Who was the first goalie ever to be sent off whilst playing for City? This happened in a 1973 Welsh Cup tie at Bangor City.

4   Tempestuous 1970s striker, sent off twice in only 21 appearances for Cardiff.

5   In February 1979, this tender 17-year-old right-back became the youngest player ever dismissed for City, on his second League appearance. It all 'kicked off' during a Second Division fixture at Ewood Park, Blackburn.

6   Another right-back; this one has the 'distinction' of becoming the first City player to be sent off on his League debut for the club, a Fourth Division game in September 1987 at Wrexham.

7   Permed stopper who skippered City to promotion in 1988. Red-carded for stamping on Swansea's Paul Raynor in an Easter Monday clash at the Vetch in 1989.

8   This one is a little bit different. Who was sent off *against* City in the famous FA Cup tie against Leeds in January 2002?

9   Who chalked up two dismissals against Swansea in the same season in 2008/09?

10 Big midfielder, on loan from Charlton, who managed to acquire two red cards in a mere 6 appearances for us in 2006/07. 'Goodnight, John Boy!'

11 Can you name this chunky left-winger who made only 14 League starts for City? He was dismissed at Brisbane Road in October 1972 in what proved to be his final game for us before returning north.

Round
5

What's In a Name?

When we were in school, nobody seemed to go by their right names, not even the girls.

Even today we have mates with names like Yogi, Bonehead, Numbnuts and What-Not. These are real people, we promise you.

Maybe it's a Cardiff thing.

See how many of these City stars you can get from the nicknames below. We haven't made these up – promise. These are genuine nicknames from reliable sources.

1   Can you tell us who was sometimes known around the dressing room as 'Bosun'?

2   So if 'Benno' crossed for 'Gibbo' ... who would that be then?

3   Can you name the first black player ever to captain Cardiff City, and what was his popular nickname?

4   Who was 'The Gentle Giant'?

5 Paul Maddy – gifted midfield youngster from the same era
– was always bouncing around like a kangaroo apparently,
giving rise to which nickname?

6 More a nickname shared amongst the fans than in the
dressing room this one – but can you recall the somewhat
ironic moniker given to one Steven Charles Lynex who
graced the Ninian Park turf in the late 1980s?

7 Which fringe member of the 1983 promotion squad was
always known an as 'Possum'?

8 H?

9 How is Constantinous Micallef better known?

10 Which Welsh international centre half, signed from
Swansea City in 1987, bore the dubious nickname
of 'Speedy'?

11 In 1978/79 our top scorer Gary Stevens (11 goals) bore
such a striking resemblance to a certain Torquay-based
hotel owner that he earned which nickname?

FA Cup
Replay

Yeah, we know – we did a round on the FA Cup in *Never Mind the Bluebirds* volume I. But we thought this most prestigious of competitions, the oldest football tournament in the world no less, deserved another look.

Plus we had a few questions left over ...

1   How did City 'win' the Cup in 1999?

2   Rob Earnshaw has famously scored hat-tricks in all divisions and all competitions. His FA Cup hat-trick came in November 2000, in a televised Sunday game. Against whom?

3   Until 2008, City's best post-war performance was reaching the fifth round, which they did in 1972, 1977 and 1994. They got there again in 2010. Who knocked us out in those years? (We also reached this stage in 1949, 1950 and 1958, but we're guessing you won't remember that far back ...)

4   Which team did City play away in the third round of the
    2006 and 2009 competitions, but at two different grounds?

5   And which lower division team did City play in successive
    FA Cup ties (two different seasons, mind) in 2002?

6   How many of City's 2008 FA Cup final team can you
    name? What about the five subs? (There were also two
    travelling reserves!)

7   Okay, enough of the Wembley day out – sometimes the
    Cup can also throw up some right nightmares. Since City
    joined the League in 1920, they have been knocked out
    by non-league sides on only five occasions – but can you
    name the five non-league teams? We will give you a clue
    and tell you that the years when this happened were
    1982, 1991, 1993 and 1995. Oh, and 1936 ...

8   It's a funny old game, Saint. What strange event occurred
    three seasons running, between 1956 and 1958? It was
    strange for two reasons. Can you tell us why?

9   In the 1990 campaign, City drew 2–2 at home to
    Gloucester City, then scraped through 1–0 away in the
    replay. Which striker scored all three goals for the Blues
    – his only senior goals for the club?

10 What happened after City drew 0–0 at Ninian Park with
    First Division QPR in the third round of that campaign?

11 In 1991, the FA introduced penalty shoot-outs to decide ties, to be played at the end of a drawn replay. So when was the only time City were involved in a penalty shoot-out in an FA Cup tie, and who did we play?

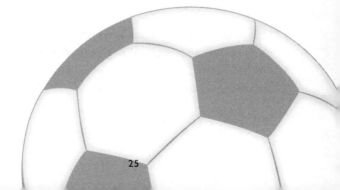

Stadium Facts & Figures

As we have said, this book is part history book, part joke book, part quiz book. Its mission is both to entertain and inform.

This round probably falls more into the 'inform' category, as we lift the lid and go behind the scenes at our celebrated venue.

1   A bit of a random start, but is it possible to get married at a football ground?

2   Can you name the famous ex-Bluebird who has a road named after him in the vicinity of the stadium?

3   One of the hospitality areas within the stadium shares its name with another football ground. No, it's not the 'Vetch Lounge' ... do you know which other ground we are talking about?

Dear Mr Tan,

We think you should call the stadium " The Never Mind the Bluebirds Stadium."

We think that's a really good name!

David and Gareth

Compass Group • **Cardiff City Stadium** • Leckwith Road, Cardiff CF11 8AZ
T: 0845 365 1155 • F: 0845 365 1166
E: enquiries@cardiffcityevents.co.uk • www.cardiffcityevents.co.uk

4 How did Roger Andrews contribute to the environs of the new stadium?

5 Which American rock band played a gig at the stadium on 12 June 2013?

6 What innovative new product was introduced at the stadium in 2012 to help raise funds for local children?

7 Which of the following items must not be brought into the ground – mobile phones, cans or cigarettes?

8 True or false – part of the Cardiff City Stadium is named the 'Bob Bank?'

9 Can you name the 'new' pub outside the new stadium?

10 On what date was the statue of Fred Keenor unveiled?

11 Finally – without looking – what is the postcode of the new stadium?

Round

8

Wartime Days

The year 2014 sees the centenary of the outbreak of the First World War.

This seemed an appropriate opportunity to recall some aspects of wartime football which have touched the club down the years. A bit of a tough round this perhaps, but it's full of interesting facts and figures. We have tried to keep these questions in a loosely chronological order …

1 In a distant echo of the legendary football match played out on No Man's Land between British, French and German troops on the First World War battlefields, Cardiff City also played a couple of friendlies against fierce rivals over Easter 1919. Who were our foes for these games?

2 Having turned professional in 1913, which City legend joined the 'Footballers Battalion' (17th Middlesex) at the outbreak of the First World War and was twice wounded in action?

3   Cardiff City escaped relatively lightly in terms of
    First World War casualties. But can you tell us which
    important figure in the club's history was lost to us
    during that conflict?

4   Can you name the 1990s City star who led significant
    fundraising activities for a memorial to be erected to
    honour the 17th and 23rd Middlesex battalions on a site
    close to where both battalions suffered grievous losses
    on the Somme? (The memorial, the first of its type
    remembering the Footballers' Battalions, commemorates
    the sacrifices made during the Great War.)

5   Not exactly a wartime-related question, but what feature
    made up part of Cardiff City's home kit before being
    permanently replaced in 1919?

6   Moving forward in history now, we discover that, as soon
    as the Second World War began in 1939, Football League
    games were quickly suspended (after only three fixtures).
    But which Anfield legend was one of a number of guest
    players for Cardiff City's 'first team,' which continued to
    operate during those dark days?

7   Which obscure Merseyside team beat Cardiff City in the
    final of the Welsh Cup in 1939?

8   Walter Parker was chairman of Cardiff City during its
    finest hour, as they defeated Arsenal to win the FA Cup
    in 1927. But what other high office did he occupy after he
    had severed his links with the club?

9   Penrhiwceiber-born Billy Baker, who made a few
    appearances for the club prior to the Second World War,
    and talented youngster Billy James both had unhappy
    times at the hands of which nation during the Second
    World War?

10 In 1945, there was much admiration for the heroism
    shown by the Russians during the war. Which famous
    Russian side visited Ninian Park for a friendly in
    November of that year? They were also honoured with a
    civic reception from the Lord Mayor of Cardiff.

11 Wales played 17 so-called 'wartime internationals'
    between 1939 and November 1946. These were usually
    against England but, towards the end of the hostilities,
    also featured Scotland and – on 4 May 1946 – Northern
    Ireland. This game ended in a 1–0 defeat for the Welsh
    in front of an amazing gate of 45,000 at Ninian Park. No
    caps were awarded for wartime internationals – but, if
    they had been, which two City players would have earned
    them for taking part in that game?

Round
9

Never Going Back, Again

Right then, back to more frivolous matters now. We had discussed writing an entire book based only on Fleetwood Mac songs, y'know.

We talked about the Langston debt as an 'Albatross' around our neck, remembered the 'Little Lies' we had told to get off work early for midweek matches and even contemplated our 'Dreams' of promotion to the Premier League. Plus of course, countless transfer 'Rumours' over the years.

Nah, terrible idea, we thought. Let's just stick with this round. Can you identify the following Boomeranging Bluebirds?

1   Lanky centre-back who joined us for a loan spell from Swansea in 1986. A year later, he joined us permanently from the same team. (Also features elsewhere in this book, by the way.)

2   Lanky striker who came to us on a loan spell from Fulham in 1987. Two years later, he joined us permanently from the same outfit.

3 Moustached utility man who left us for Swansea City in 1985; then rejoined us from Newport County in 1989.

4 Another moustached man, he captained us to promotion, left for St Johnstone, and then came back for not one, but two loan spells.

5 Right-back or (less successfully) right-midfielder, he joined us from Hereford United, left us for Birmingham City, rejoined us from Sunderland, then (after being released) left us again – to rejoin Hereford United. All this occurred between the late 1980s and the mid-1990s.

6 Left-sided utility man who left us for Oxford United in 1988, then rejoined us from the same club a decade later. Strangely, he then left us to rejoin ... Oxford.

7 Geordie striker who joined us from Newcastle United, left us for Sunderland, came back on loan, then back again on loan, then rejoined us permanently. Then took a gamble by heading off for Ipswich Town – phew!

8 Popular striker who left us for West Bromwich Albion, then rejoined us from Forest. An extra two points if you can remember the two teams he played for in between.

9 Name these two players who came back for unproductive trial spells. One of them was a winger from the early 1970s who played a part in a famous goal, before leaving for Bridgend Town – then rejoining us on trial a few years later ...

10 ... and the other was an inconsistent midfielder who left us for Swansea City in 1983 – then rejoined us from Hereford for a pre-season trial spell in 1989. It didn't come off, and he went to Malta.

11 Several ex-City players of the early 1970s Scoular vintage rejoined the club as coaches during Richie Morgan's early months as manager, in 1978/79. How many of them can you name? About four, we think.

Round

10

On the Spot

We decided that, as we did in the first volume of *Never Mind the Bluebirds*, we'd build in a little breather for those overworked brain cells of yours.

Last time we ran a round of 'Dad or Chips' where we set you agonising choices to see if you preferred Ninian Park over the Cardiff City Stadium, home games over away games, or Danni Minogue versus Kylie!

Anyway, something along similar lines here. Eleven questions to put each of us 'on the spot' and find out just what sort of City fans we are. So give us *your* answers to these questions.

Once again, there are no right or wrong answers, but we have included our responses in the Answers section just for fun. By all means quiz yourself on these teasers too. We think this round might take you the longest as you all deliberate over your choices. Some are more difficult than you might think. Have fun!

David's answers appear first in the answers. We always go David first, then Gareth; have you noticed? We even stand that way in pubs. Ant & Dec think they invented it, but no, they pinched the idea from us when they saw us at the bar in The Corporation.

1 First Cardiff City Home Game

2 First Cardiff City Away Game

3 Favourite All-Time Cardiff City Player

4 Favourite Current (2013) Cardiff City Player

5 Player of the Year: 2013

6 Favourite Cardiff City Goal

7 Favourite Cardiff City Moment

8 Favourite Kit (Home)

9 Favourite Kit (Away)

10 Favourite Terrace Chant

11 If I could change one thing about Cardiff City it would be ...

Round

11

And it's Cryptic City, Cryptic City FC!

This book is nothing if not varied. We hope you agree. We have tried to include questions and rounds for all ages.

But in this round – well, it's little more than wordplay really. We just wanted to irritate you!

We think we may have achieved that here. (We hope you kept your receipt when you bought this book.)

1   Can you name this 1980s City coach, who was certainly a jolly _____?

2   In the early 1990s, how could City play this _____ and still win?

3   Still in the early 1990s, which moustached winger came and stayed for a day?

4 City often kept a clean sheet when this gangly stopper played for us (on loan) in 1993. Who would that be?

5 Tell us the left-footer in the late 1990s who liked to play with his fast, sporty ones.

6 In the Lennie Lawrence era, which centre-half did something before that?

7 Who was our tallest-ever goalie, whose brothers were in films (maybe)?

8 … and the unproductive Noughties striker who was often in the soup?

9 Tell us the name of this little forward, formerly a flying milkman?

10 Maybe this on-loan goalie (play-off disaster) should have played for coastal clubs.

11 And finally, you'll be relieved to hear, reveal to us the identity of this on-loan midfielder (play-offs era) who should have played for spa town clubs?

Cardiff Born & Bread

'And when I dies I'll be …'

In this round, we have done a bit of digging around to uncover a range of facts about the links between Cardiff City and the city itself. It's a meandering tale, but this round could appeal to the local historian in you. Is Cardiff City woven into the very fabric of the city? See what you think.

Schools football has always been big in Cardiff. Ex-City boss Richie Morgan played in this fixture at Ninian Park.

1 Which Cardiff high school did John Toshack attend?

2 Joe Ledley is from which part of Cardiff?

3   City legend Nathan Blake was born in Cardiff – is that
    true or false?

4   There are few people with more passion for the club than
    director Steve Borley. Famously, he once lived extremely
    close to Ninian Park. Can you name the road?

5   ... and can you tell us the name of the parks team he once
    helped to form?

6   Talking of parks football, can you name the long-standing
    cup competition held annually in the parks of Cardiff?
    There is a City connection ...

7   Back in the days before websites and message boards,
    football fans developed the phenomenon of fanzines
    – fan run magazines which featured all kinds of useless
    gossip and speculation. Which of the following was
    not a Cardiff City fanzine: *The Thin Blue Line*, *Watch the
    Bluebirds Fly*, *Never Say Dai*?

8   What is the connection between bread and rum?

9   Cardiff City take much pride from being the only Welsh
    team to win the FA Cup. But how many of those 1927
    heroes were actually Welsh?

10 Which part of Cardiff did 1920s goal-scoring legend
    Len Davies come from?

11 Cardiff City's fanbase has always stretched way
    beyond the city boundaries, of course. In the 1970s
    and '80s, Cardiff City Supporters' Club existed
    alongside another Supporters' club. Can you
    name that Pontypridd-based organisation?

O BLUEBIRD OF
HAPPINESS NO.1

UNFORTUNATELY 50 PENCE

CITY SAD AS TONY
OPTs TO QUIT....

CARDIFF CITY FC ^un OFFICIAL
FANZINE

Whatever happened to these guys?

Great Days
(The 'El Clarkico' Round!)

We are guessing that, if you have bought – or been given – this book, then you are something of a Cardiff City fan. It's a strange gift if you are not.

But we are also guessing that you have something of a passing interest – even knowledge – of the history of the club. You remember the big games, the Glory Glory nights; the famous Cup clashes and bristling promotion campaigns.

Or do you?

These questions all revolve around some of the most famous matches in the history of Cardiff City. But, outside of the headlines, we wonder how much you really know about these epic encounters. These are harder questions than you think.

1   We all remember that Scott Young stabbed home that dramatic winner against Leeds United in January 2002. Many of us recall that it was Graham Kavanagh who scored the other. But who scored for Leeds that day?

2   Men of a certain age will point to the night when
    'they were there' to see Cardiff City beat the mighty
    Real Madrid on 10 March 1971. BBC commentator
    Idwal Robling described it as 'Cardiff City's greatest
    fixture ever.' 'El Clarkico!' Here's one for you: what
    colour kit did the famous Spaniards wear that night?

3   OK then, if that wasn't our most famous game, then
    surely this one was. 23 April 1927. The rest is history,
    as they say. To this day, Cardiff City remains the only
    Welsh team to have won the FA Cup. We all know that
    Cardiff City beat Arsenal at Wembley that day – but who
    did they beat in the semi-final?

4   Winning the cup, of course, also allowed Cardiff City
    to boast another distinction. Can you tell us this often
    overlooked achievement?

5   Right then, who remembers season 2012/13? Think so?
    Who scored the last goal of our League season?

6   A bit more up to date now. Who would have emulated
    Fred Keenor to lift the famous FA Cup trophy had
    Cardiff City beaten Portsmouth at Wembley in 2008?

7   For the 2012/13 season, Cardiff City famously
    (infamously?) changed their home shirts from blue to
    red, also introducing a new badge as part of a 'rebranding'
    of the club. Who were the first opponents to face the
    red-shirted Bluebirds?

8   Another question about semi-finals now. Well, sort
    of. City famously beat QPR in 2003 to finally return
    to the second tier of English football. But who did
    we beat in the two-leg 'semi-final' to reach the
    Millennium Stadium?

9   Of course, not all memorable matches are played out
    at giant stadiums on big occasions, or even before the
    watching Sky millions. If you followed Cardiff City
    in the 1980s and '90s, you had to lower your sights
    a little when looking for glory. For example, on
    2 May 1988 City clinched promotion from the old
    Fourth Division (now League Two) by beating Crewe
    Alexandra 2–0. The 47,000 diehards who turned out for
    Real Madrid had shrunk to 10,125 for this one – easily
    the largest crowd of the season, when gates normally
    hovered around the 4,000 mark. Still doesn't seem that
    long ago to us. Anyway, who scored the goals that day?

10 Finally, a typical tale from the adventures of Cardiff City:
a packed ground, the glare of the floodlights, a day in the
spotlight as Cardiff City reached the semi-final of the
European Cup Winners' Cup against HSV Hamburg on
Wednesday 1 May 1968. To set this occasion in context,
this would be the equivalent of, say, Ipswich Town playing
Bayern Munich in the semi-final of the Europa League.
A crowd of 43,000 saw Cardiff City literally throw away
the chance of glory as the ball skidded out of our goalie's
hands into the net ... during stoppage time, added due to
a pitch invasion. Like we say, all very Cardiff City. Now we
won't insult you by asking you to name the keeper ...
but who scored that goal?

11 In 1976, Cardiff City beat Hereford United to (virtually)
clinch promotion to the old Second Division, in front of
35,000 fans. Can you name all 35,000? Whoops sorry,
misprint there. Can you tell us the unlikely City scorers
that day?

The Good, the Bad & the Bellamy

Over the years, we all have our favourite players.

David Collins modelled his own playing style on Jason Perry (though maybe without the pace) and Gareth still flaps his arms like Cohen Griffith as he runs. Yes, there have been many heroes down the years.

In recent years, the great Craig Bellamy has been something of a talisman for us, inspiring the fans to raise their voices and his colleagues to raise their game.

We feel his contribution therefore merits a round of his own. But be warned, our lovable hero may be a Golden Boy to us, but things haven't always gone to plan for the Trowbridge Tearaway. Over the years, CB39 has been no stranger to controversy, so we have snuck in a few of his more 'colourful' adventures here …

[Gareth: 'Is snuck a proper word?']
[David: 'Yeah, proper Trowbridge grammar that is!']

1   During the 2002/03 season, Craig was sent off in a
    Champions League game for Newcastle United against
    Inter Milan for kicking an Italian international defender.
    Who was this defender, and how did he gain notoriety a
    few years later?

2   What happened when Bellars had a disagreement with
    Magpies coach John Carver just before he was due to
    travel to a European away tie?

3   Why was Alan Shearer reportedly incensed by the Good
    Fella following Newcastle United's 2005 FA Cup semi-
    final defeat by Manchester United – even though the
    Welshman was in Ireland with Celtic at the time?

4   Why did Graeme Souness announce that the Rumney
    High School product would never play for Newcastle
    United again, in January 2005?

5   What was Craig's reported response when
    Birmingham City were interested in signing him following
    the above incident?

6   What was notable about Bellamy's half-season loan at
    Celtic in 2005, in terms of winning trophies?

7   Who were the two Wales colleagues that the Trowbridge
    marksman reunited with at Blackburn in 2005?

8 What allegedly happened on a Liverpool trip to Portugal in February 2007 – and who was the other Liverpool player involved? Also what was the sequel to this incident, when both players appeared in a Liverpool win over Wigan shortly afterwards?

9 What happened when an opposing fan ran onto the pitch during a Manchester derby game at Old Trafford in September 2009?

10 Craig returned to the international scene in February 2012 after missing quite a few games due to injury. Can you name Wales' opponents that day?

11 Finally, as you can see, Craig gets some pretty bad press at times. But there is another side to him. Can you name the West African country in which he has set up a Football Foundation?

Round
15

Board
Stiff

Many years ago, the chairman, directors or owners of a football club were often little known figures.

In the last thirty years or so though, these characters seem to have taken on a higher profile.

Rest assured: as in most things, Cardiff City have not been left behind in such developments.

So come on, then. How much do you know about this band of dreamers and schemers?

(We were going to end this round with 'Freddie and the Dreamers' by the way, in tribute to our former Chair Fred Dewey [1962–72], but that would have been too corny, even for us.)

1   Who is generally regarded as the first chairman of Cardiff City?

2   Who was chairman when we won the Cup in 1927?

3   … and who was chairman when we got to the final again in 2008?

4 Which chairman of the 1920s was sent to jail, and what for?

5 At least two chairmen of the club have gone on to become president. The first one was a 1930s docks businessman, later knighted, who appointed himself as president in the mid-1950s. Who was he?

6 Who succeeded to the title of chairman when this guy became president?

7 The next name we want was another docks businessman, who moonlighted as a Justice of the Peace in the courts of Penarth and Barry, and supported the use of the birch. He also became president in the 1970s. Who was he?

8 Which former City chairman was forcibly ejected by stewards from the directors' box, and then escorted out of the ground, prior to a Second Division fixture in 1978?

9 Which City chairman was a Geordie whose first love was Newcastle United?

10 Which City chairman appointed his wife to sit on the board of directors with him?

11 And which chairman appointed his girlfriend as chief executive of the club?

Round
16

1983 and All That

You know that line about Spurs always winning the FA Cup if the year ends in a one? Well, we can top that.

Think about this ... 1983, 1993, 2003 and now of course 2013. Which team won promotion in each of these seasons? That's right, Cardiff City! Remarkable, eh? Maybe we can look forward to winning the Champions League in 2023?

That 1983 season is still regarded with much affection by many City fans. Manager Len Ashurst had failed to save City from relegation to the old Third Division (aka League One) in 1982 but, through careful shopping in the Bargain Basements and Whoops Aisles of the lower divisions, cobbled together a memorable, if tiny, squad made up of various unconnected journeymen and a handful of committed local players. Under the calming influence of skipper Jimmy Mullen, our band of heroes roared through the division to finish runners-up in 1983 – thirty years before Malky's men wrote their own names in history.

Football was very different thirty years ago. Hooliganism was rife, away kits were only worn if there was a colour clash and everyone played at 3 p.m. on a Saturday. Shirt sponsorship was years away, Cardiff City shared their ground with a rugby league team and David Collins had long hair and highlights. Ah, those were the days, eh?

If you are in your 40s now, this round will take you back to your teens. You will race to the attic to dig out your Soft Cell records, dust off your pastel-coloured shell suit and try to convince yourself that, even now, you could carry off that haircut sported by Mike Score from A Flock of Seagulls.

1 Cardiff were promoted as runners-up in 1983 as we have said. Who finished top of the division though?

2 Len Ashurst was of course the manager. Which club had he previously managed immediately before coming to Ninian Park?

3 Tough one now. In that season's squad, City had three members whose surname started with the letter H. Can you name all three?

4 From which club did City sign Godfrey Ingram?

5 The great Jeff Hemmerman swaggered his way to the top of the club's goal-scoring charts that year. How many League goals did he grab?

6 City clinched promotion by beating Orient 2–0. Who scored our goals that day?

7 The Bluebirds were famously dumped out of the FA Cup by a non-league team that season. Who were those celebrated giant-slayers?

8 Which player played in every League game that season and went on to make a total of 129 consecutive appearances?

9 Four of the squad that season played for Wales at some point in their career. Can you name the international quartet?

10 Just before the start of the season, a world-famous figure made an appearance at Ninian Park. Who was it?

11 Finally, Linden Jones and Phil Dwyer made an unusual contribution to the away game against Bradford City in February 1983. Can you tell us what that was?

Go on then, how many can you name?

Round

17

Trivia Trail

After the publication of last year's book, a detailed programme of consultation followed to gauge customer feedback. We held roadshows, focus groups and drop-in sessions, ran blogs and online forums. We encouraged written and oral responses. One of the headline indicators to emerge from this structured approach to measuring satisfaction level, was that the Trivia Trail round was in the upper quartile in terms of popularity – allowing for accepted tolerance levels in the statistical analysis and appropriate margins of error.

We also stuck it in because it's the easiest one to write.

The format is simple enough. The last letter of the first answer is the first letter of the next answer, and so on through the list. Just fill in the gaps!

1 _____ Bank

2 _____ Hatton

3 Nickname?

4 _____ Hammam

5 Sponsor

6 1927

7 Carling (Cup, that is … so we aren't looking for 'lager!')

8 Andy _____

9 _____ End

10 _____ May

11 Earnie?

Round

18

True
or False

Some of the rounds in this quiz book are quite complex, even cryptic perhaps.

Some though, are more straightforward.

Like this one, maybe. We simply want your 'true' or 'false' answers. Nothing could be simpler.

Yeah, right …

1   Former Charlton winger John Robinson joined
    Cardiff City in 2003. Despite winning 30 Welsh caps,
    he was born in Africa … wasn't he?

2   Robert Earnshaw was born in Zimbabwe.

3   John Toshack went to Fitzalan High School.

4   City signed Robbie James from Swansea City.

5   1990s speed merchant Cohen Griffith was born in
    Guyana.

6   All the players mentioned in this round so far were
    eligible to play for Wales.

7   George Best scored for Northern Ireland at Ninian Park
    in 1970.

8   Joe Ledley is actually Scottish by birth.

9   For a short while, before King Edward VII granted Cardiff
    city status on 28 October 1905, the club were known as
    Cardiff Town.

10 1970s stars Albert Larmour and Bill Irwin both won caps
    for the Republic of Ireland.

11 Don Murray was undefeated as manager of Cardiff City.

Round
19

More Cryptic City

What the heck … we are guessing you have just about got over that earlier cryptic round – oh, here we go again. Relive the agony with some more corny cryptic clues to identify these City favourites.

1　This famed 1920s stopper was a more eager player than most.

2　In general terms, a damn good centre-half from the 1950s.

3　Many rivers were crossed during the career of this 1950s centre-forward.

4　Attractive overlapping play from this 1960s full-back led many to exclaim, 'Ding-dong!'

5　Fringe 1970s forward who spent more time in these than on the pitch.

6   This little 1970s midfielder always told the barmaid,
    'I'll have a _____, darlin'' ...

7   What did Paul do in the mid-1970s, after he came?

8   Signed on a Tuesday, vanished on a _____?

9   Lots of love from the Ninian faithful went out to this
    French-sounding centre-half from the 1970s.

10 Another 1970s centre-back, this local one thought playing
    for the City was going to be like a holiday camp.

11 There was always something a bit fishy about
    Durban's goalkeeper.

59

It's a
Family Affair

Phew, after that last brain-twisting round, we get back to
conventional questions here.

Right then, hands up – who went to their first-ever football
match with their dad?

Yeah, of course we did; almost everyone went to their first
game as a trembling youngster with their dad or uncle, and in
such ways the dye becomes cast.

Don't worry though, this isn't a round devoted to the
adventures of our fathers. In this round, we invite you to
contemplate the family connections at Cardiff City down
the years. Easy one to start, right?

I Whose brother made 18 appearances for us in the early
   1980s? This Welsh under-21 international also played
   for Newport County, Merthyr Tydfil, Ebbw Vale, Inter
   Cardiff/Inter Cabeltel, Cwmbran Town and Grange
   Harlequins. He also enjoyed a role as Swansea City's
   youth coach.

2   Ex-City manager Richie Morgan's Cardiff City career included 4 games alongside his brother in 1972/73, as City narrowly avoided relegation. Can you name the sibling?

3   Glamorous brothers who starred for us in the 1980s. One a tricky winger, one a classy defender. Think Manchester City ...

4   Who were the last father and son to play for Cardiff City? (Not together, mind.)

5   Can you name Craig Bellamy's son?

6   City's 1930s right-back Arthur Granville's grandson played for the Bluebirds in the 1990s. Intriguingly, he shared the same initials as his grandad – but not the same surname. Can you name him?

7   Legendary footballing brothers John and Mel Charles both played for Cardiff City in the 1960s. Which one joined the club first?

8   Take another look at question 1. Their dad played in a band at the old 'Bluebirds Club', as well you know. Go on clever clogs ... name the band!

9   Uncle and nephew? We have that covered too ... Len Attley enjoyed (or maybe 'endured') two seasons for us in the mid-1930s, which would make his nephew ...?

10   Jimmy Blair/Doug Blair – what is the connection?

11   Finally, a twist in the trail. These two players shared the same name, but were not related in any way whatsoever! One was a fleet-footed ex-postman, and the other was a bald and fearsome centre-half. Both appeared for City in the 1990s. Can you name them?

Badge of Honour

Listen, it's not the role of this book to go over the rights and wrongs of the whole 'rebranding' thing.

Yeah, you might spot the odd reference to our opinions on it amongst these pages, but there are other, more appropriate platforms for that debate, we reckon.

But tinkering with the badge is nothing new. Although the issue of the new badge has sparked fierce debate, it was not until 1958/59 that the team started to wear a badge on their shirts. Since then, they have always worn one – but its form has changed over the years more than you might realise.

Let's discover how much you recall. Extra points if you have **any** of these badges tattooed on your torso, by the way.

1   What badge featured on Cardiff City's shirts in the 1925 and 1927 FA Cup Finals?

2   What colour cross appears on the badge worn in the 2008 FA Cup Final?

3   And to complete the Wembley trilogy, which badge adorned our shirts for the 2012 Carling Cup Final at Wembley?

4   From 1965–69 the home shirt featured no 'badge' at all, but merely a single word, as if written by hand, in white letters. What was that word?

5   By the time Real Madrid came to town in 1971, the single word had been replaced by … what?

6   The famous 1975–80 kit of blue with a white and yellow stripe featured a simple version of the Bluebird logo. But something unusual happened to the badge on that kit. What was it?

7   Cardiff City have never bothered with stripes – have they?

8   We expect you know that the new badge introduced in 2012 features the words Cardiff City FC and 'Fire & Passion' (why not 'hwyl?') but what other expression features on this badge?

9   Would you ever find the badge elsewhere on the kit?

10 Cardiff City's obsession with badges reached new heights in season 1973/74. How did that manifest itself, exactly?

11 Finally, this whole badge thing is nothing new really, is it? The club began life as Riverside AFC in 1899, wearing a groovy kit of chocolate and yellow quarters. So was the badge worn on the chocolate side … or the yellow?

Proper badge. Proper footballer.

Round
22

Gimme a
C ... 'C C!'

Drawing inspiration from a popular terrace chant, we have
produced a set of clues which will lead you to a particular set
of answers. If you then take the first letter of each answer they
spell out a famous phrase.

   It's not as complicated as it sounds, honest ...

1 First up, we are looking for the surname of this 1927 hero
   who, at the time, was the youngest player to appear in an
   FA Cup Final.

2 Get that one, did you? OK, next up, we need the surname
   of this gifted utility player from the 1970s who also played
   for Swansea City.

3 Another FA Cup Final connection here; which
   ex-Bluebird captained Southampton to a famous victory
   over Manchester United in 1976?

4   Can you name the tough-as-teak Cardiff legend who
    ended his career at Rochdale?

5   One of the strangest transfer deals involving Cardiff City
    featured a payment of £200,000 in 1982 to the San Jose
    Earthquakes. Nine weeks later the same player was
    transferred back to the same club for exactly the same
    amount. Can you name the player?

6   We both remember this fragile-looking young winger
    from the late 1980s who left us for Hereford in 1991.
    He was Player of the Year at Colchester United in 1997
    and also had a spell with Barry Town. Yeah, we remember
    him well enough, question is ... do you?

7   'Double the ...' Nah, that would be giving the game away!
    Much maligned City striker Chris Pike topped the club's
    goalscoring charts three seasons out of four, back in the
    1990s. In fact he is tenth on the club's all-time scoring list.
    Who did we sign him from?

8   Fans of a certain age will recall our silky defender from
    the late 1960s, Steve Derrett. We sold him eventually in
    1972 to which club in the far north of England?

9   This Ulsterman has the distinction of being the first
    Cardiff City goalkeeper to be sent off.

10   Easy one now. Is this guy a Jack or a Bluebird? Though we think really his heart lies in Real Sociedad.

11   Lastly, we need the surname of this ex-Wales skipper who played many times at Ninian Park but never in the blue (or even the red!) shirt of Cardiff City. He had a curious spell as director/manager here for a while though. Another who has managed the Jacks, by the way.

Round

23

Behind
the Scenes

The following questions are about the unsung heroes and
loyal bootroom and back-office staff. We think you might
be surprised how well you do here. (Incidentally, in Danny
Gabbidon's day, the back office wasn't a room where the
admin staff worked; it was the room where he had his back
seen to …)

1 Can you name the famous 1920s trainer, a former Welsh
   international? Newtown FC's ground is named after him.

2 Who was the Central Boys' club coach who
   joined City's staff in the late 1960s, and remained for
   some thirty-five years?

3 Tell us the name of the physio who saved Phil Dwyer's life
   at Gillingham in 1975.

4 Can you name 'Number Two' to Len Ashurst, who also served as physio and coach? He even (briefly) had a spell as City's manager.

5 Who was our curly haired 1983 scoring sensation who later began treating Ninian injuries instead of sustaining them?

6 Still on the treatment table, who was Director of Football for a few weeks in 1995 who tragically died on the operating table?

7 Another one from our dark days of the 1990s. Can you name the figure who was successively team manager, Director of Football, caretaker-manager and Director of Football (again)?

8 Who was our long-serving secretary (mainly during the 1960s) who also had a famous uncle?

9 And our club secretary from the 1990s who was a famous '60s referee?

10 Still in the 1990s, this blonde Commercial Manager was romantically attached to owner Samesh Kumar. Who was she?

11 And who is our occasionally naughty Noughties matchday announcer? 'Support the Boys and Make Some Noise!'

A Word from
Our Sponsors

It's ok, this is not a page of adverts. Rather it's a round *about* adverts.

Or, more specifically, shirt sponsorship.

In the grand scheme of things, shirt sponsorship is a relatively modern phenomenon, having only really hit us in the 1980s. Before that, footballers such as Kevin Keegan were reduced to merely 'splashing it all over' in adverts for Brut Aftershave.

Nowadays, however, adverts are 'splashed all over' the shirts themselves, as kit manufacturers battle with shirt sponsors to attract the eye. Replica shirt sales is big business these days of course, and we know of many a wardrobe packed with row upon row of shiny tributes to the likes of Merthyr Motor Auctions, Airways Cymru and Vans Direct.

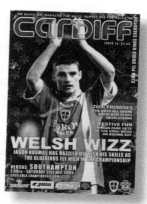

Football in the new millennium. How many logos can you spot hidden in this picture?

What, these names mean nothing to you? Oh dear. This may not be the round for you, then.

1 Obvious one to start. Who were Cardiff City's first-ever shirt sponsors?

2 Can you name another brewery to have featured on Cardiff City shirts?

3 City have regularly attracted sponsorship from local firms, but can you tell us the only Welsh word to appear on a Bluebirds shirt?

4 Which sponsor stayed on our shirts the longest?

5 What's black and white and red all over?

6 Which pop group once sponsored Cardiff City shirts?

7 Go on then. We have to ask this one. SuperTed – what's that all about then?

8 The club turned the clock back during 1998/99 by introducing the white sleeves which had characterised our home shirts for many years during the 1930s, '40s and '50s. Can you remember who the shirt sponsors were for that shirt? Think Jason Fowler, Kevin Nugent etc. if it helps. (Some of us have spent years trying not to think about Kevin Nugent!)

9   Here's a good 'un. Can you name the City player whose
    name appeared on the front AND back of his shirt?

10 Many of you will get this one, so we will have to be strict.
    Who sponsored our shirts in the 2008 FA Cup Final?

11 And who were the shirt sponsors for the Carling Cup?

Round

25

Never Mind the Word Search!

We got this idea while waiting in the dentist's, reading all the magazines they leave out.

Kids love a word search – so we have hidden a fictitious City line-up of eleven recent City stars in the grid below. See if you can find the stars. They don't all follow on around the grid one after another, mind. That would be too easy.

Watch out for the odd red herring too … there are at least two City managers hiding in the grid, for example.

You will need a pencil and a 5-year-old for this round. The task is to find the fantasy line up on the following page hidden in the grid below it:

Marshall

Gunter   Loovens   Blake   Matthews

Ledley   Koumas   Ramsey   Bellamy

Mason   Chopra

```
M  A  C  K  A  Y  A  R  P  O  H  C  B  O  B
N  I  N  I  A  N  P  A  R  K  T  O  S  H  E
I  L  E  G  I  W  D  M  C  Y  E  L  D  E  L
H  O  G  C  C  F  C  S  H  F  L  J  N  B  L
M  O  K  C  C  F  C  E  O  V  H  O  L  L  A
N  V  T  O  N  I  F  Y  P  N  X  N  S  A  M
R  E  T  N  U  G  C  O  R  T  O  E  O  K  Y
Y  N  C  C  H  U  D  S  O  N  B  S  U  Y  E
O  S  A  M  U  O  K  D  I  P  U  B  A  D  E
U  J  B  M  A  T  T  H  E  W  S  X  R  M  S
J  A  S  O  N  N  O  T  K  O  U  M  O  S  S
A  C  L  U  E  Y  M  R  A  Y  A  R  A  B  J
C  I  T  Y  L  E  E  L  L  A  H  S  R  A  M
K  N  M  T  B  V  I  A  B  A  L  L  S  U  P
```

Round

26

Guess the Year

'That's all you ruddy think about isn't it ... Cardiff Blinking City!'

Sound familiar? Does this sound like the breakfast table in your house, or the rantings of your maths teacher after another 'must try harder' session?

We know it's not true of course. We know that you are a rounded, well-read individual whose hobbies and interests are numerous and varied. We know you keep up with current affairs, politics and world history. Just see how many of the clues below you can negotiate, for example, to identify the years in question. That'll learn them, eh? Oh ... and just to help you out, we have stuck in a few City references too – not that you need them, of course.

I   The Queen turns 25; the King dies ... and Peter Sayer scores a cracker to knock Spurs out of the FA Cup.

2   Charles marries Diana, Bob Champion triumphs at
    Aintree and Bobby Sands starves himself to death in
    The Maze prison. Peter Kitchen tops the Bluebirds
    goalscoring charts with 19. City hold West Ham 0–0
    to escape relegation in the final game.

3   Charles divorces Di. 'Football Came Home'. Carl Dale is
    top man this time, with 30 in all competitions.

4   City fan Neil Kinnock becomes leader of the Labour Party
    and Cardiff City acquire Karl Elsey and Nigel Vaughan in a
    bizarre five-man swap deal from Newport County.

5   Tricky one here … Heath Ledger posthumously wins
    an Oscar for his role as The Joker in the *Dark Knight*.
    Lady GaGa also reaches No.1 in the pop charts with
    'Bad Romance'. At London Road things go equally gaga
    for Cardiff City as, thanks to goals from Joe Ledley (2),
    Jay Bothroyd & Peter Whittingham, the Bluebirds hold
    what seems to be an unassailable 4–0 half-time lead. But
    in an amazing second half, Peterborough pull back four
    goals to draw the game 4–4. When did all this malarkey
    take place then?

6   The year of the Falklands War. Spurs win the Cup
    – Len Ashurst begins his first stint as manager of
    Cardiff City.

7 The year of the Space Odyssey? Cardiff City also boldly reach new horizons by signing their first million-pound player this year. But which year? (Extra point if you can name the player.)

8 The USA invades Iraq, Ozzy and Kelly Osbourne hit the top of the charts with 'Changes' and Robert Earnshaw bags his record 31st League goal for Cardiff City.

9 The USSR send Laika the dog into space and Elvis Presley stars in *Jailhouse Rock*. Danny Malloy stars in all 42 League games for Cardiff City, but couldn't help us avoid relegation to Division Two.

10 Benny Hill, Slade, Rod Stewart and Dave & Ansil Collins have No.1 hits this year. Cardiff reached the final of the FA Youth Cup. (What, Dave Collins had a hit single?)

11 Los Angeles hosts the Summer Olympics and Liverpool win the European Cup in Rome. Alan Durban takes over from Jimmy Goodfellow as manager. No truth in the rumour that we try to sign George Orwell in this year, mind.

Round

27

The Fearful 1950s

Having just got through the war, the 1950s remained a period of great uncertainty. Rationing continued, as did National Service, and there were wars in Korea and Egypt (Suez).

In Canton, however, a far more important fear gripped the Ninian faithful: fear of relegation from the First Division. To be fair, there were also successful promotion campaigns to get to the top flight, in 1952 and (in footballing terms, still in the 1950s) 1960. But you knew all that, didn't you?

We have stretched the boundaries a little in this round, as we also propose to test you on the immediate post-war years, which brings in the record-breaking Third Division South campaign of 1947. Here we go, then. Get on your thinking caps – or even your cloth caps.

I   Who were the City managers when the Bluebirds:

   a)   won Division Three South in 1947?

   b)   finished runners-up to Sheffield Wednesday in Division II in 1952?

   c)   finished runners-up to Aston Villa in Division II in 1960?

2   And who were the captains during those three campaigns?

3   Oh, almost forgot to ask: what about the leading scorers?

4   In April 1953, City recorded their highest-ever official
    attendance at Ninian Park. Who were the League leaders
    who visited that day, and what was the attendance,
    and the score?

5   City had some interesting results that season.
    In February, they played host to Man City. In April,
    they had successive fixtures versus Man Utd (away) and
    Liverpool (home). Can you remember any of the scores?

6   Who did City beat 3–2 at Ninian in the penultimate game
    of the 1955 season to stay up? And who was the debutant
    who scored for us?

7   What was the score when City faced the same opponents
    at Ninian early the following season?

8   Which City players of this era did the following:
    a)   wrote an autobiography called *I Lead the Attack*?
    b)   played part-time and worked as a coalminer,
         but later played for England?
    c)   was a lay preacher as well as a winger?

9   Who did we sign those three players from?

10   Who went from Barry Town to Arsenal in 1953? And
     from which non-league outfit did Bill Jones arrive as
     coach in 1957?

11   These two lesser-known City players were both in the
     Wales squad for the 1958 World Cup finals. One was
     a long-punting goalie from Aberdare, who also took
     net-bursting penalties for the reserves, and lost his
     first-team place at City after arriving late for a game.
     The other was a North Walian forward who swiftly
     returned to Wrexham after only one season in Cardiff.
     Can you name them?

Great
Expectations

This round deals with those Bluebirds who promised much – then, for one reason or another, seemed to deliver comparatively little. Most of them moved on to pastures new, but none of them really set the world alight. One or two, having got the big-money move away from Ninian Park, proved to be a 'fish out of water', and gradually faded from view. Were all these players really underachievers? Discuss …

I   Not strictly a City product, this tall right-winger from the 1960s was considered an underachiever, because he had already played in the League for Birmingham. Virtually unplayable on his day – but he didn't have enough of them. He moved on to Bury, and within a couple of years of leaving City, he was plying his trade in South Africa. Who was he?

2   From the same era, this Glaswegian joined as a youngster, scoring many goals once he was put in at centre forward. Moved to Arsenal in 1967, but had packed in the game within a few years after getting through a host of different clubs.

3   Another Scot, he formed a partnership up front with Derek Showers in the team that got to the 1971 FA Youth Cup final. Unfortunately, within a couple of years, he was playing for Bath City (and then Bridgend Town). His name … ?

4   Dashing young winger from Port Talbot who supplied the cross for that Brian Clark goal against Real Madrid. A couple of years later, he was terrorising defences at places like Weymouth and Salisbury City, turning out for Bridgend Town in the Southern League. He was … ?

5   This winger-cum-striker scored a famous goal against Spurs in 1977, got a big move to Brighton and then – became a golf club steward in Preston.

6   Another 1970s forward, this dribbler from the Gwent valleys scored a sensational goal against Palace to keep City up in 1974. Appeared to have a big future in the game; alas, his real future was as a milkman in his native Panteg.

7   Decent all-action midfielder who left City in 1987 after falling out with Frank Burrows, spurning League football for the delights of working as a car mechanic in Tredegar. He did come back later, but not for long.

8   Lanky but fragile-looking dribbling winger who volleyed
    a great goal at Ninian against Brentford in 1989.
    We thought he looked good, but he only turned out to be
    good enough for Hereford, Colchester and Exeter.

9   Elegant-looking defender who went from being, in the
    mid-1990s, a future Wales international and Premier
    League player to – Exeter City. What went wrong?

10 Tall and willowy striker who got a dream move to Premier
    League Coventry after only a handful of appearances
    for City in 1997. But his career went onto a side-track
    which led only to the likes of Wigan and Tranmere.

11 This last entrant was one of 'Three Musketeers' who
    together scored regularly in the late 1990s for the City
    youth and reserve sides, alongside Rob Earnshaw and
    Christian Roberts. The third, alas, ended up playing for
    Inter-Cardiff, Barry Town, Aberaman and Caldicot Town.
    Anyone remember his name?

A Tale of
Two Cities

What the Dickens is going
on here, we hear you cry …

If you are a City fan of
a certain vintage, you may
recall the days when our
REAL derby foes came
from the west of England.
Cardiff and Bristol – Bristol
and Cardiff. Surely a more
fitting rivalry, as two cities
of a decent size, than
Cardiff and that little place
on a hill by the Mumbles.
So, this round deals with
former Bluebirds who
also had dealings with
one or other of the two
Bris'l sides – Blue Wurzels,
you might call them …

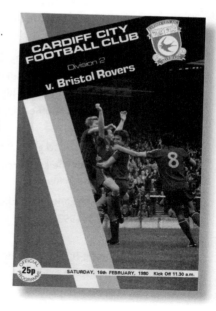

CARDIFF CITY
FOOTBALL CLUB

Division 2

v. Bristol Rovers

OFFICIAL PROGRAMME 25p

SATURDAY, 16th FEBRUARY, 1980   Kick Off 11.30 a.m.

1 Whisper this question quietly, but which influential figure in the Bluebirds' early days was actually from Bristol?

2 Which centre half joined us for a £30,000 fee from Bristol City in 2000 (big money for us in those far-off days), but only made a handful of appearances for the first team? (Think: son of somebody famous.)

3 Which Cardiff-born forward joined Exeter after being released by City in 2000, but later regularly hit the back of the net – and often the bar – at Ashton Gate?

4 Who was the lanky midfielder we signed from City (Bristol City, that is) in 1996?

5 Going back a bit further now. Who was the ex-Rovers (two spells at Eastville) right-back we signed in 1987 from Brentford, and who was the high-flying ex-Rovers goalie we obtained (from Sheffield United) in 1993?

6 Which goalie left us to go to Roverzz in 1972, and which centre-back went the same way in 1997?

7 Who was the elegant midfielder who came to City from Ashton Gate in 1993?

8 And which long-haired midfield general left us for Bris'l City in 1989?

9 Who managed both City and Bristol City in the 1990s?

10 Two players who appeared in the First Division for City in the early 1960s had come from the Roverzz — one of them a Welsh international striker, the other a cricketing goalie. Can you name them?

11 Who were these two wingers from the same era (early 1960s)? One joined us from City in 1959, played in our promotion team of 1960, but moved on to Eastville in '61. The other joined us from Rovers in '62, but moved on to Bristol City in '63 after being our top scorer in his only season at Ninian Park. He was renowned for his fierce shot.

Ex-Cardiff City boss. Ex-Bristol City player. Perfect.

Between
the Wars

Finally, we take a last dip into the pages of history here as we test your knowledge of events which occurred between the two world wars – that is, the period 1918–39. We weren't able to dig out our ticket stubs from any of these games, sorry.

1   In a 1924 Home International game between Wales and Scotland at Ninian Park, what was unusual about the two captains – and who were they?

2   By what margin did City lose the 1924 League title? Who finished ahead of them?

3   City's final game that year was at St Andrews, Birmingham. Who took a crucial penalty for City midway through the second half – and who saved it for the (Brummie) Blues?

4 Who was our utility player (playing at right half that day) who was robbed of the ball by Sheffield United's Fred Tunstall, in an incident which led to the only goal of the 1925 FA Cup final?

5 Who was the City outside right absent due to pleurisy at the time of the 1927 final – and who was his replacement who was cup-tied for the game?

6 What was unusual about City's statistics when they were relegated after finishing bottom of the First Division in 1929?

7 Which FA Cup winner came back to City in the disastrous 1933/34 season – and where did City finish that year?

8 Which forward – City's leading scorer in the 1931 and '32 seasons – was capped by Ireland, despite City's lowly status in the League at that time?

9 And which centre forward was our leading scorer in the last two seasons before the war?

10 Which popular local player was a virtual fixture in the side at outside right during the late 1930s?

11 Which Troedyrhiw product made 3 League appearances for us at outside right in 1939, before reinventing himself as a left half after the war?

We thought we'd visit on 8 February.
We are sure of a warm welcome.

The 'Current Affairs' Round

1 Malky went to Carrow Road and cried 'Let's be 'aving you.' So the answer we wanted was Norwich City.

2 The game took place on 16 April 2013, fifty-three years to the day when we last won promotion to the top flight when beating Aston Villa 1–0, thanks to a goal by Graham Moore. City wore an all-white kit that day, by the way. They had worn that kit a few times in games leading up to that day apparently, and thought the kit could bring them luck. Changing colours to a lucky kit? Wouldn't happen these days, would it…

3 Burnley. This game had added significance as it clinched the Football League Championship for us. So that's the League Championship, FA Cup AND Charity Shield we have taken out of England so far.

4 The Premier League is the most-watched football league in the world. Figures released in 2013 indicate that it is broadcast in 212 countries.

5 Nicky Maynard.

6 Cardiff City signed Chilean international Gary Medel, nicknamed 'El Pitbull' for £9.5m from Sevilla.

7 City winger Craig Conway replaced Robert Snodgrass after 66 minutes. Ex-City striker Kenny Miller scored for Scotland. David Marshall was a non-playing substitute.

8 Cypriot businessman Mehmet Dalman.

9 For the 2013/14 season, Cardiff City changed the logo from the puzzling 'Malaysia' to the slightly more fathomable 'visit Malaysia'.

10 Sam Hammam. A colourful quote, even by Sam's standards. This was just one example of the new-found love between Sam and Tan which blossomed when the two finally cleared up their financial fallout in July 2013.

11 Craig Bellamy. He was taken off in the second half as City went for broke to try and rescue the game. West Ham scored again moments later...

1 'The **greatest** team in football, the world has ever seen.' Interestingly this may not have been as easy as it seems, for most teams sing '...by far the greatest team, the world has ever seen.' Not as good, is it?

2 '...Graham Kavanagh' (We would also have accepted 'Leo Fortune West', but the Kav line works better.)

3 '...Barmy Army.' Sneaky, ain't we? There was a time when the chant of (say) 'Eddie May's Barmy Army' was followed by a 'remix' with the lyrics 'Ooh Ah – Barmy Army. Ooh Ah – Barmy Army.' It's a haunting melody.

4 'Willie Willie Willie Willie Anderson'. A classic glam-rock hit from the 1970s.

5 'He puts the ball in the net. Fraizer Campbell will always score goals.' (Sung lustily to the tune of 'The Entertainer' by Scott Joplin – as used in the Robert Redford/Paul Newman film *The Sting*.)

6 Well, he does 'what he wants', of course. A song beautifully remixed in a 2013 encounter with Ipswich Town, when well-known gambler and ex-City star Michael Chopra warmed up on the touchline – only to be serenaded with 'Michael Chopra ... he bets what he wants.' Priceless. The only time we have witnessed a terrace song attract a round of applause from the rest of the crowd.

7 Routledge – a reference to ex-City loan signing Wayne Routledge, who made 9 appearances for the Bluebirds in November 2008 while on loan from Aston Villa. He later signed for Swansea City to further cement his place in our hearts.

8 'La, La-La, La-La.' Sheer poetry.

9 'You'll never ban a City fan.' The ill-fated voucher scheme of the 1980s; the ID card from the 1970s; Stay Away from Derry; twenty City fans at Torquay. Don't let the system grind you down. If Bob Dylan had written a City song, this would have been it.

10 '…and nod one in.' Don't walk off with the idea that witty terrace banter is a modern phenomenon. This one comes from the late 1940s, in tribute to goal-scoring hero Stan Richards.

11 '…walking round the pitch.' Former City chairman Sam Hammam (for whom the word 'character' was doubtless invented) introduced the seemingly unthinkable practice of walking around the pitch at Ninian Park **while the game was going on**. Honest! He would do this against the likes of Leeds United, strolling past the away fans and waving, sending them absolutely mental. Not surprisingly, the home fans loved it. This is one of many terrace chants which are based on the Gap Band's 'Oops Upside your Head.' Other ditties to use this tune include 'Who needs Cantona when we got Stantona?' (a reference to our ex-striker from the early 1990s, Phil Stant) and 'Ooh Ah Paul Millar.' Rhyming 'Millar' with 'Cantona' always seemed a little contrived to us. But hey, it's only rock 'n' roll, right?

View from the Dug-Out

1   After being shown the door following boardroom changes at Ninian Park, Scoular managed Newport County. He also acted as scout for Swansea and Newcastle.

2   Coventry City.

3   Lennie Lawrence.

4   Cyril Spiers was at the helm from April 1939 to June 1946 and again in 1947 for a further seven years. But in the meantime, Billy McCandless had a short spell in charge from June 1946 to November 1947.

5   Alan Cork.

6   Fred Stewart.

7   We won't accept Alan Durban or Richie Morgan. The answer is actually Russell Osman, who made 15 appearances in the 1995/96 season and then became manager for one whole month in November 1996. (These were very dark days…)

8   Complicated question but a straightforward answer. Coventry City.

9   Jimmy Scoular. And yeah, we know – your Dad hasn't been to a game since.

10 Bellshill – which is in North Lanarkshire, 10 miles south-east of Glasgow. ('Scotland' would actually have done, come to think of it.)

11 The late Jimmy Andrews managed Cardiff City between 1974 and 1978. Robin Friday constantly referred to the boss as 'Archie' after Archie Andrews – a ventriloquist's dummy

used by Peter Brough in a radio and television show in the 1950s and '60s, 'Educating Archie'. Not quite sure how ventriloquism worked on the radio, but there you go.

Class Dismissed!

1 Jimmy Nelson. He conceded a late penalty in the game, which Manchester City converted to win 3–2. Nelson claimed he always had one eye on the ball …

2 The winger sent off was Colin 'Rock' Hudson. Later, our forward Steve Mokone and their defender Harry Griffiths were both dismissed as well, for the novel crime of throwing mud at each other!

3 Northern Irishman Bill Irwin, who coincidently had begun his career with the other Bangor, in the Irish League. He went off in the first leg of the Welsh Cup final, which City lost 1–0 at Farrar Road.

4 Robin Friday. Who else!

5 Linden Jones, after an altercation with Rovers left-back John Bailey. Bailey was also dismissed, and City won the game 4–1.

6 Phil Bater. Wrexham was one of his former clubs.

7 Terry Boyle. City were 1–0 up at the time, and managed to hold on for a 1–1 draw. And we're not sure if stamping on Paul Raynor really qualifies as a red-card offence…

8 England international forward Alan Smith, after a tussle with Andy Legg. Smith's furious team-mate Robbie Fowler then claimed Legg was play-acting. Whatever happened to that Fowler geezer afterwards?

9 Stephen McPhail.

10 Simon Walton, little-remembered by City fans for anything other than those two dismissals. After the second, on his way up the tunnel, he booted the digital timekeeper's board

and put that out of action! (NB If you don't understand
the reference to the 1970s family orientated TV show
The Waltons, ask your mum!)

11 The disappointing Alan Foggon. The game was drawn 0–0,
and while it was Foggon's last, it was also Phil Dwyer's first.

What's In a Name?

1 Phil 'Joe' Dwyer. Something about him steering the ship?

2 That would be a cross from Dave Bennett, crashed into the net by Roger Gibbins. Bliss.

3 Clive Charles. In 1974–75 full back 'Charlo' became the first black player to captain Cardiff City. And according to Gilo's brother Paul, it IS true what they say…!

4 John Charles of course – though his actual name was William John Charles.

5 Joey.

6 'Lethal' Lynex. Steve might generously be described as a 'trier.'

7 Winger Paul Giles has carried this nickname since childhood. Your average possum (a small, furry little critter) spends much time scurrying about before leaping up into a tree. Apparently, this was a regular feature of Baby Gilo's life as a small child and the name just stuck.

8 Legendary City club man Harry Parsons became City's kit man after being recruited by Jimmy Scoular in the mid-1960s to look after the youngsters.

9 'Tarki'.

10 Nigel Stevenson. A tall defender, but perhaps not known for his pace.

11 'Basil', after Basil Fawlty. Stevens' 11 goals included 5 in 5 games at the start of the season (which meant only 6 during the rest of the season!).

FA Cup Replay

1 Well, Cardiff City didn't win the Cup – but the city of Cardiff did. The FA decided to stage the Cup finals at Cardiff's Millennium Stadium while Wembley was being rebuilt. The next seven finals (from 2000 to 2006 inclusive) were all held there. Cardiff also hosted the League Cup Final, Play-Off finals and even the Charity Shield in those days. We reckon they should have held the Boat Race on the Taff too.

2 Bristol Rovers.

3 In 1972, City lost 2–0 at home to then-mighty Leeds; in 1977, we lost 2–1 at home to Everton; and in 1994, we lost 2–1 at home to second-tier Luton (we were in the third tier, mind). In 2010, we lost 4–1 at Chelsea. (Incidentally, for completists, in 1949, we lost 2–1 at Derby; in 1950, we lost 3–1 at Leeds; and in 1958, we lost 2–1 at Blackburn.)

4 Arsenal, of course, losing 2–1 at Highbury in 2006, and then getting stuffed 4–0 in a replay at the Emirates (after a 0–0 draw at Ninian) three years later.

5 Tranmere Rovers.

6 The starting XI was: Peter Enckelman, Kevin McNaughton, Roger Johnson, Glenn Loovens, Tony Capaldi, Peter Whittingham, Gavin Rae, Stephen McPhail (capt), Joe Ledley, Jimmy-Floyd Hasselbaink, Paul Parry.

The five subs were: Michael Oakes (GK), Trevor Sinclair, Darren Purse, Aaron Ramsey and Steven Thompson. (Darcy Blake and Riccy Scimeca also travelled with the squad, but did not make the final 16.)

7 The teams who gave us those black days were Dartford in 1936; Weymouth in 1982; Hayes in 1991; Bath City in 1993; and Enfield Town in 1995. That Hayes game was played at Brentford's Griffin Park ground, incidentally – so maybe it at least felt like we lost out to a League team.

8 City drew Leeds United in the third round, away from home, three seasons on the trot. The odds against that happening are 2,000,376 to 1 – that's over 2 million to 1! Even stranger, City won 2–1 on all three occasions.

9 Morrys Scott.

10 All the takings were stolen by someone who had worked in the club's office. The cash was later found half-buried on a mountainside up the valleys, and the thief was successfully prosecuted.

11 In 1998, after two 1–1 draws against Reading, we lost the fourth round replay 4–3 on penalties at the Madejski Stadium.

1 Yes. Cardiff City Stadium is licensed to provide rooms for civil ceremonies and civil partnerships.

2 Fred Keenor, 1927 FA Cup-winning captain was honoured by naming 'Ffordd Fred Keenor' in his memory.

3 The 'Ricoh Suite' can be used for various functions and shares its name with the Ricoh Arena (former home of Coventry City).

4 Roger Andrews of Llantwit Major is the sculptor of the 2.7m high statue of Fred Keenor which stands in the car park.

5 Bon Jovi.

6 In 2012, the 'Cardiff City Community Pie' was launched. It's a homemade cottage pie that, when purchased, will see Levy Restaurants make a donation to the Cardiff City Community & Education Foundation. A pie with a conscience? Whoever would have thought it, eh?

7 Ground regulations state that knives, fireworks, smoke canisters, air-horns, flares, weapons, dangerous or hazardous items, laser devices, bottles, glass vessels, cans and poles must not be brought into the ground. Mobile telephones are permitted within the ground, provided that they are used for personal and private use only. So all those clips you have posted on YouTube are gonna have to be removed, sorry. Smoking is not permitted inside the ground, though cigarettes in themselves are not banned. So the answer to the question is … cans. We are pleased to see that flares are banned by the way, but wouldn't want that to

extend to tank tops. Half our wardrobes would be ruled out if that came into force.

8   False – we have a Canton Stand and a Grange End but no Bob Bank. In fact, officially, there was no Bob Bank at Ninian Park either. If you study all the club's official literature, the huge terrace which ran the length of the old stadium is always called something like the Popular Bank or even the Popular Terrace. Nobody ever called it that of course, and to generations of City fans, it was always the Bob Bank, so-called because it used to cost a shilling (5p) to stand there – a shilling being colloquially known as a 'bob'. You can't buy anything for 5p now.

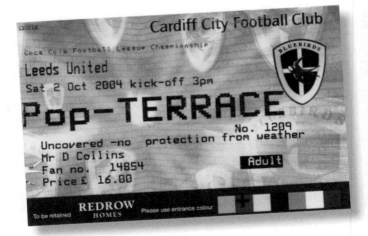

The Popular Terrace?

9 The Sandmartin.

10 10 November 2012, prior to our 2–1 victory over Hull City.

11 CF11 8AZ. In recent years the match day programme has also been known as 'CF11.'

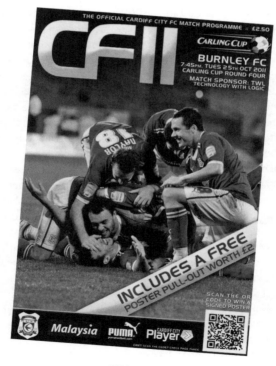

CF11.

Wartime Days

1 Swansea Town. The Jacks came out on top at the Vetch on Good Friday (2–0), while the Bluebirds got their revenge in Cardiff on Easter Monday (3–0). Attendances at these games were 12,000 and 18,000 respectively. These games were billed as 'wartime friendlies' as, although the war ended in 1918, League football did not resume until 1919.

2 Fred Keenor. At the end of the war he returned to Cardiff and made his first appearance for Wales in the Victory Internationals.

3 Lord Ninian Crichton Stuart MP. He was the second son of the Marquis of Bute. He was amongst five individuals who stood as guarantor for the £60 annual ground rent of a site for a new ground at Sloper Road in 1910. In his honour, the club named the new ground Ninian Park. He was guest of honour for the opening game, a friendly against League champions Aston Villa held on Thursday 1 September 1910. He even took the kick-off for this match (at 5 p.m.). He was eventually killed by a sniper's bullet at the Battle of Loos in Belgium in October 1915. The only fatality amongst the players was reserve full-back Tom Witts. John Wilson – son of City founder Bartley – also lost his life while serving with the 17th Welsh Regiment in France in 1917.

4 Phil Stant. Back in 1982, Stant was billeted at Aldershot and playing part-time for Reading, before Argentina's military junta took a course of action that would change his life. He was just 18 when he boarded the QE2 and headed to the South Atlantic to take part in the Falklands conflict. Phil Stant scored over 40 goals for us in the early 1990s.

5 Black socks.

6 Bill Shankly.

7 South Liverpool beat Cardiff City 2–1 at The Racecourse Ground, Wrexham. We must confess to knowing little about South Liverpool, other than that they won the cup at this, their first attempt. These were unusual times for the Welsh Cup as the following season, 'Wellington Town' beat the Jacks 4–0 at Shrewsbury to take the cup. In 1969 Wellington Town became Telford United. Things returned to normal after the war, with the 1946/47 final being contested by those established giants of the Welsh football scene, Chester City and Merthyr Tydfil.

8 Walter Parker became Lord Mayor of Cardiff in 1944.

9 Japan. (They were both prisoners of war.) 1927 hero Earnie Curtis was also captured by the Japanese and became a prisoner of war from 1941 to the end of the Second World War.

10 Moscow Dynamo, who beat Cardiff City 10–1 that day.

11 Alf Sherwood and Roy Clarke. A tricky one that, we admit.

1 Nigel Stevenson.
2 Chris Pike.
3 Roger Gibbins.
4 Paul Ramsey.
5 Ian Rodgerson.
6 Mike Ford.
7 Michael Chopra.
8 Robert Earnshaw. He went from West Bromwich Albion to Norwich City, and from thence to Derby County – then on to Forest.
9 Nigel Rees.
10 Paul Maddy. He played in one pre-season friendly, for one half, at left-back. We thought he looked okay there…
11 Brian Harris (assistant manager), plus Bobby Woodruff, Brian Clark and Don Murray.

On the Spot

David	Gareth

1 Cardiff City versus Hereford United. 1968 Welsh FA Cup Final (second leg). City won the match 4–1 to take the trophy 6–1 on aggregate. John Charles played for Hereford.

Boxing Day 1988. City drew 2–2 with Swansea City, Jimmy Gilligan gave us a 2-goal lead after only 6 minutes but the Jacks grabbed a draw. An attendance of 10,675 for this High Noon shoot-out by the way.

2 Again, the Welsh Cup provides the answer. 20 February 1973 found me at Somerton Park to see Cardiff City beat Newport County 3–1 in front of an impressive crowd of 11,350.

Gillingham in that same 1988/89 season. We won 2–1. Amazing to think that Gillingham were regular opponents back then.

3 Rather than write an essay, I am going to just say … Nathan Blake. Jason Perry and Joe Ledley were in the frame too. And Jimmy Gilligan … oh yes, and Jeff Hemmerman, and …

I always appreciated the effort made by Carl Dale. He starred in a very poor side indeed. Would like to have seen how he fared with better players around him.

4 CB39. An absolute inspiration. Worth the admission money alone some days.

Mark Hudson has been an important player for us – but my favourite is Kev McNaughton, as he has been here longest.

5 David Marshall. He seemed to make vital saves in so many games that we then went on to win, and even almost scored against Bolton Wanders. I also enjoyed watching Kimbo.

Again I would go for Huds, though I agree that Marshall was worth a shout.

6 It has to be, doesn't it? John Buchanan against Swansea 1980. Read about it, Google it. 40 yards out etc., etc …

Blakey's curler against Manchester City in the FA Cup fourth round tie in 1994 springs to mind, though I reckon the most important goal was scored by Andy Campbell in 2003 against QPR. That goal took us out of the dungeons at last and shoved us back to where many always felt we should have been.

7 Reaching the FA Cup Final. I am in my 50s, so the FA Cup still matters to me. As the final whistle blew I was overcome with emotion. Away trips to Torquay, relegation battles from the 1970s, memories of FA Cup Grandstand … and now it would be our turn. Wish my Dad could have been there.

I loved that Scott Young moment against Leeds in January 2002.

8 From 1975 to 1980 Cardiff City wore a fantastic all-blue kit with a white and yellow stripe down the side. Perhaps it's my age but this, for me, remains the iconic Cardiff City kit.

I am not really a kit man … though I used to like the blue one they wore …

9 That fabulous 1970 kit also had an away version, which was all yellow with a corresponding blue and white stripe. You can still buy this, you know. But my favourite is probably the black away kit from around 2007 – loosely based on the colours of the St David's cross flag.

I can live with red – as an away kit.

10 'Cardiff City. Cardiff City FC. The Greatest Team in Football, the World has Ever Seen.' The fact that we are clearly not just makes this song all the better for me.

11 I know you can see this coming but … can we have our blue shirts back, please?

'Who needs Cantona when we've got Stantona.' Very witty, I thought. My No. 2 is 'Always Shit on the English Side of the Bridge.' (Appropriate for a 'number two', eh?)

Go back to a blue home kit, red away kit and move back to Ninian Park.

And it's Cryptic City, Cryptic City FC!

1 Jimmy Goodfellow ('For He's a Jolly...' oh, you got it. OK).
2 Lee 'Baddeley'.
3 Wayne Fereday ('For a Day?').
4 Alan Knill ('NIL').
5 Anthony Carss.
6 Spencer 'Prior'.
7 Tony Warner.
8 Andy Campbell.
9 Earnie!
10 Steven Bywater.
11 Oh, Danny Danny, Danny, Danny, Danny, Danny Drinkwater.

1 Canton High. Before that he was at Radnor Road Junior School.
2 Fairwater.
3 True. Many sources quote his Newport upbringing – but he was actually born in the capital.
4 St Donat's Close, right alongside the old ground.
5 Llanrumney Mad Dogs!
6 It's the City Supporters Cup. We are grateful to Allen Stroud, Vice-Chairman of the Cardiff & District Football League, for his confirmation that this competition is still running. Sadly he was unable to recall David Collins' only appearance in the competition for Pentwyn Dynamos in 1987. Shocking memory some people have, eh?
7 *Never Say Dai*. This was a Newport County magazine. Witty title, given the upheaval that club faced in the fanzine era of the 1990s.
8 'Captain Morgan Rum – the right rum for today's tastes' was advertised on the old Bob Bank roof for many years before being replaced by 'Braces Bread – the bread for all seasons.'
9 Just three. Fred Keenor, Ernie Curtis and Len Davies.
10 Splott.

11 Adar Glas Caerdydd Supporters Club (run by Mair Daniel.) 'Adar Glas' is slightly clumsy Welsh for Blue Bird. We reckon it should be either 'Aderyn Glas' (Blue Bird) or 'Adar Gleision' (Blue Birds.) We won't dwell on that though. There was even a third club in existence at the time by the way, based in Barry. There has always been one in Maesteg too, of course.

Great Days (The 'El Clarkico' Round!)

1 Mark Viduka (he gave Leeds the lead in the 12th minute but, after that … well … y'know).

2 Real Madrid's usual kit was all white. No badge, no sponsor's logo, no 'Bale II' emblazoned across the back. Just all white. Cardiff City's blue shirt from 1970 was usually accompanied by white socks and shorts. So to avoid a clash that night Real Madrid wore … all red.

3 Reading.

4 City were able to compete for the 1927 Charity Shield. The match was held on 12 October at Stamford Bridge. City met amateur side Corinthian. The game ended in a 2–1 win for City – we also won the Welsh Cup that year. As things currently stand, this treble is unlikely to be repeated.

5 On an amazing last day of the season, City drew 2–2 away to Hull City. Nicky Maynard scored an injury-time penalty moments after David Marshall had saved one at the other end. Priceless. The draw took Hull up at the expense of Watford.

6 Steve McPhail.

7 City wore red at home for the first time in a pre-season friendly against Newcastle United (and won 4–1), but the answer we wanted was Huddersfield Town. The Bluebirds met the Terriers in their opening fixture on Friday 17 August 2012. Huddersfield, inevitably, wore blue.

8 Bristol City. Cardiff City kept a clean sheet in all three play-off games that year. A feat previously unperformed. Again, the sort of fact that gets forgotten these days.

9 Kevin Bartlett and Brian McDermott. (Yes – the former Reading boss.)

10 Franz-Josef Hoening put in a harmless shot from thirty yards which City keeper Bob Wilson fumbled over the line in the dying seconds. Anyone who answered Uwe Seeler go back to jail … do not pass Go. Do not collect £200.

11 Doug Livermore and Alan Campbell. Livermore only scored 5 goals for City, while Campbell was even less prolific with just 2.

The Good, the Bad & the Bellamy

1 Marco Materazzi. Three years later, he allegedly made abusive comments to Zinedine Zidane in the World Cup final, leading to Zidane headbutting him and being sent off.

2 He threw a chair at Carver and refused to travel to the game. After Bobby Robson eventually calmed the situation, he did travel.

3 Bellamy reportedly sent abusive text messages to Shearer, gloating in Newcastle's defeat. He later claimed his mobile had gone missing at the time, and that he never sent them. And his dog had eaten his homework…

4 Souness claimed that Bellamy had refused to play out of position on the right wing in a Premier League game at Highbury. (Funny to think that he was still considered to be an out-and-out striker in those days.)

5 'I don't play for shit teams.'

6 He won a Scottish Cup winners' medal – the first trophy of his professional career. He had to wait until 2012 for the next one, against us at Wembley!

7 Manager Mark Hughes and Robbie Savage.

8 He allegedly hit left-back John Arne Riise with a golf club. In the Wigan game, Bellamy pretended to hit Riise with an imaginary golf club after scoring.

9 As he was being 'escorted' from the pitch by stewards, Craig appeared to slap him.

10 Austria.

11 Sierra Leone. The Craig Bellamy Foundation runs Sierra Leone's only professional football academy.

1 Sid Nicholls, the former Welsh international rugby player.
2 Walter Parker.
3 Steve Borley.
4 Watkin Williams, chairman straight after we won the Cup, in 1927/28. He was a Cardiff docks ship-owner who was jailed for conspiring to sink his own ships in an insurance scam.
5 (Sir) Herbert Merrett.
6 Ron Beecher.
7 Fred Dewey. His son Vernon also sat on the board.
8 Stefan Terlezki – who, after becoming Conservative MP for Cardiff West in 1983, strangely complained about the behaviour of football hooligans!
9 Bob Grogan.
10 The much-unloved Tony Clemo. His wife was Linda.
11 Samesh Kumar. Although it should be pointed out that his girlfriend, Joan Hill, was widely perceived to be a highly efficient chief executive of the club (Joan sadly lost her battle against cancer in May 2013).

1983 and All That

1 Portsmouth finished top, with 91 points. City came second on 86, ahead of third-placed Huddersfield Town on 82.

2 He managed Newport County from 1978–1982 before joining Cardiff City.

3 Jeff Hemmerman, Bob Hatton ... and Steve Humphries (goalkeeper).

4 San Jose Earthquakes (USA).

5 22.

6 John Lewis and Dave Bennett.

7 Weymouth beat Cardiff City 3–2 after being 2 goals down. FA Cup exit to a non-league team in a promotion year. Unthinkable!

8 Roger Gibbins.

9 Phil Dwyer earned 10 caps, Paul Bodin won 23, Andy Dibble won 3 caps and Keith Pontin (who played in 4 games that season) won 2. Linden Jones made the squad for the game against Brazil but never won a cap. Hands up all those who think Paul Bodin was twice the player Dwyer was?

10 Pope John Paul II addressed 33,000 people at Ninian Park.

11 Following a first-half injury to City keeper Andy Dibble, Dwyer went in goal until half-time (keeping a clean sheet) before Linden Jones took over between the sticks for the second half. Linden conceded two goals. City lost 4–2 with goals from Gibbins and even Dwyer – possibly the last 'goalie' to score for City!

Trivia Trail

1 Bob.
2 Bob!
3 Bluebirds.
4 Sam.
5 Malaysia.
6 Arsenal.
7 Liverpool.
8 Legg – Legg, Legg. (Drat, three words!)
9 Grange.
10 Eddie.
11 Earnshaw.

Earnie! 'Nuff
said …

True or False

We enjoyed this round. Sneaky edge to it, isn't there?

1   True. He was born in 1971 in Bulawayo, which was in Rhodesia then, but it's now Zimbabwe.
2   Not quite … he was actually born in Zambia. Close, though you wouldn't want to walk it.
3   Nope … Cantonian. Don't get those two mixed up if you are strolling through Canton or Grangetown.
4   False – James had three spells at Swansea, but we actually signed him from Bradford City.
5   True.
6   True – Cohen 'declared himself' Welsh in order to satisfy requirements in force at the time that teams playing in Europe had to field a certain number of 'home-grown' players. As a UK passport holder, he could claim to be Welsh.
7   False. Best never played at Ninian Park for Northern Ireland.

8 Rubbish. Despite his Celtic connections, Joe is as Cardiff as a Clark's pie!

9 False. They became Cardiff City on 5 September 1908. Immediately prior to that they were known as Cardiff Riverside, having begun life as simply Riverside. Watch this space though for when they simply become 'Cardiff' ... or even 'Cardiff Dragons?'

10 False. They are both Ulstermen. Irwin is from Newtownards and Larmour hails from Belfast.

11 True...or rather False. We are not sure. He never actually managed Cardiff City so technically he is undefeated! Though we reckon 'False' is the more correct answer. Or maybe true. Oh, you sort it out!

1 Fred Keenor. ('Keenor' than most…?)
2 Stan Montgomery.
3 Trevor Ford.
4 Gary Bell.
5 Derek Showers.
6 Willie Carlin.
7 Paul Went.
8 Robin Friday.
9 Albert Larmour.
10 Keith Pontin.
11 Lee Smelt (what – fish smell, don't they…?)

It's a Family Affair

1 David Giles.
2 Peter.
3 Dave and Gary Bennett.
4 We are guessing you all recall John Toshack but what about his son Cameron, who started just one game against Wrexham? 1991? Oh come on, you're not even trying...
5 Ellis Bellamy is the son of the great Craig. He has been included in various young Wales squads and plays for Cardiff City's youth academy.
6 Andy Gorman.
7 Mel joined us in February 1962 and John joined us in the summer of 1963 – for a mere £20,000.
8 Alan Giles played with 'The Grange-Enders'!
9 That would be Brian Attley – utility player from the 1970s.

10 Right, let's get this right. Jimmy Blair played in the 1925 FA Cup Final against Sheffield United and won 6 caps for Scotland while with Cardiff City. He was born back in 1888! (Like we said, 'part history book, part joke book, part quiz book'.) His son Doug was a key player in our 1952 promotion as City reached the old First Division. He played in 216 League games in total for the Bluebirds.

11 John Williams … and John Williams.

1 The Lord Mayor and Corporation of the City of Cardiff allowed Cardiff City to wear the coat of arms of the City at Wembley. (Similarly, Manchester United wore the badge of the Manchester County Football Association in the 1957 and 1963 FA Cup Finals.)

2 Gold – though we will also accept yellow. The complete badge featured a bluebird 'flying' across the St David's flag, which features a gold (or yellow) cross on a black field.

3 That would be the long-standing Bluebird within a shield and the words 'Cardiff City FC' above the shield, and 'Bluebirds' below on a type of sash or scarf. This is still regarded by many as the 'traditional' badge of Cardiff City, though, all is not always as it seems.

For example, an early version of this design occupied the shirts in 1985 – featuring gold letters and no daffodil/dragon decorations. If you look at the badge though in – say – 1983 you will see that the daffodil and dragon above the shield are drawn in a different style from more modern versions. The daffodil, for example, is much scruffier. The badge also calls us Cardiff City 'AFC' back then, whereas we became Cardiff City 'FC' according to later designs. In recent seasons the badge became 'framed' within a shield-type-arrangement but in earlier years it simply sat on the shirt itself, so to speak.

4 'Bluebirds'.

5 A bluebird on a white background. The background changed to yellow in 1980.

6 It changed sides. Traditionally the badge has always sat on the left-hand side of the shirt (if you were wearing it). For some reason, that kit placed it on the right. The 2008 FA Cup Final badge sat in the middle of the shirt. As far as we know, the badge has never been on the back of the shirts (though in recent years a Welsh Dragon flag has featured on the back).

Stripes on the badge. We weren't making it up, see.

7 Well, yes, in around 1971. They adopted the red, white and
   black-striped away kit, and even a red-and-blue Barcelona
   style 'third kit' at one point. But in terms of badges, the logo
   used to feature a bluebird badge on a blue-and-white-
   striped background.

8 'Est 1899'. No points if you said 'Established in 1899',
   'Est in 1899' or even 'Est. 1899', for there is no full stop after
   the abbreviation of 'established.'

9 Yeah, lots of versions
   of the kit see the badge
   on the shorts …
   the red kit of 2013
   for example.

10 The programme
   featured the club
   crests of all twenty-
   one of their rivals in
   the Second division –
   including Manchester
   United.

11 Yellow – on the left if
   you were wearing it.

Ernie **C**URTIS
Brian **A**TTLEY
Peter **R**ODRIGUES
Phil **D**WYER
Godfrey **I**NGRAM
Chris **F**RY
FULHAM

CARLISLE
Bill **I**RWIN
TOSHACK
YORATH

Which spells out ... oh come on, how much help do you need here?

Behind the Scenes

1   George Latham. Newtown's ground (in his hometown) is called Latham Park.

2   Harry Parsons, known to most as 'H'.

3   Ron Durham. We did think of having a round based on CCFC people with the same names as English counties. But unless we sign Jack Wil(t)shire, that might prove a pretty thin round.

4   Jimmy Goodfellow.

5   Jeff Hemmerman.

6   Now a lot of people don't remember this, but it's true. His name was Bill Caldwell, and he was supposed to work in harness with newly appointed team manager Kenny Hibbitt, but he died (during a routine operation) almost before he had his feet under the table. As to who, exactly, Bill Caldwell was – well, we've no idea. Any information would be welcome.

7   Kenny Hibbitt.

8   Graham Keenor. Not Fred's son, by the way, which is a common mistake – as Fred did also have a son called Graham. But they're not the same person.

9   Jim Finney, who had refereed the 1962 FA Cup final and in the 1966 World Cup finals.

10 The late Joan Hill, later on the commercial staff (briefly) at Spurs.

11 Ali Yassine, also author of the amusing memoir *Was it Something I Said?*

A Word from Our Sponsors

1 'Whitbread Wales' in 1983.

2 Buckley's Brewery back in the late 1980s. We will also allow you 'Brains Beers', who sponsored a barely used white top in 1996/97.

3 Cymru. As in 'Airways Cymru,' whose name illuminated City's jazzy Admiral shirts from 1985 to 1987.

4 Cardiff City were grateful for the kind support of the *South Wales Echo* from 1992 to 1997. A different shirt every year, naturally.

5 Well, as any manufacturer of Christmas crackers will tell you, it's a newspaper. In terms of Cardiff City shirts though, the *South Wales Echo* appeared across a unique red, white and black-striped away shirt (third kit?) in the days of Nathan Blake and other 1990s fashion icons. A great shirt. Indeed, a cracker, you might say. Let's move on…

6 Champions of 'Cool Cymru,' the Super Furry Animals added their name to a plain blue shirt which the club only used in the now-defunct FAW Premier Cup during 1999. This was an unusual ensemble to say the least, featuring the badge from the 1927 FA Cup Final and a retro-looking lace-up collar. Groovy.

7 SuperTed was a Welsh fictional anthropomorphic bear character created by Mike Young. SuperTed became a popular series of books and led to an animated series produced from 1982 to 1986. SuperTed's bright red costume (stick with it, honest…) featured a flame-type yellow logo. You may find this hard to believe, but that logo

appeared on the home shirts of Cardiff City AFC in 1984, as Young's company Siriol Productions invested in the club.

Mike Young also designed the huge animations featuring the likes of Robin Friday, Scott Young and Brian Clark which decorate the current stadium. (Siriol is Welsh for cheerful by the way, but as only the logo appeared and not the word 'Siriol', the answer to Question 3 still stands!)

8 The Sports Café. They had a branch down the Bay, but it didn't really last the pace after capturing the public imagination in the early days. Much like Jason Fowler maybe.

9 Why its Peter Thorne of course! Thorney was a regular name on the team sheet (not to mention the score sheet) between 2001 and 2005, when our shirt sponsors included ... Ken Thorne World of Cars. Ken Thorne also sponsored a rare green away kit in those days, by the way.

10 'Comms Direct.' The design also featured a 'CD' logo. Only half a point if you didn't get that bit.

11 Malaysia.

```
M  A  C  K  A  Y  A  R  P  O  H  C  B  O  B
N  I  N  I  A  N  P  A  R  K  T  O  S  H  E
I  L  E  G  I  W  D  M  C  Y  E  L  D  E  L
H  O  G  C  C  F  C  S  H  F  L  J  N  B  L
M  O  K  C  C  F  C  E  O  V  H  O  L  L  A
N  V  T  O  N  I  F  Y  P  N  X  N  S  A  M
R  E  T  N  U  G  C  O  R  T  O  E  O  K  Y
Y  N  C  C  H  U  D  S  O  N  B  S  U  Y  E
O  S  A  M  U  O  K  D  I  P  U  B  A  D  E
U  J  B  M  A  T  T  H  E  W  S  X  R  M  S
J  A  S  O  N  N  O  T  K  O  U  M  O  S  S
A  C  L  U  E  Y  M  R  A  Y  A  R  A  B  J
C  I  T  Y  L  E  E  L  L  A  H  S  R  A  M
K  N  M  T  B  V  I  A  B  A  L  L  S  U  P
```

Easy when you know how, eh?

1 1977 – the Queen's Silver Jubilee. Elvis Presley died.
2 1981.
3 1996. Cardiff City finished 90th out of 92 that year – 2 off the bottom. Just above Torquay United and Scarborough. Think of this when we are playing Chelsea and Manchester United this season … (Baddiel and Skinner released 'Football's Coming Home'.)
4 1983.
5 2009 – just. That posh horror show took place on 28 December 2009.
6 1982.
7 2001 (*2001: A Space Odyssey*, classic 1960s sci-fi film). The player in question was Graham Kavanagh, who we signed from Stoke City.
8 2003.
9 1957 – Malloy was also ever-present in 1959 and 1961.
10 1971. City lost the FA Youth Cup Final to Arsenal. Revenge for 1927? Hardly…
11 1984. Durban took us from the Second Division to the Fourth … that would be the Championship to League 2 these days. In 1986 he left football to run an indoor tennis club in Telford.

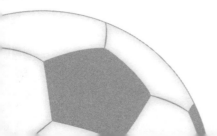

The Fearful 1950s

1 Billy McCandless; Cyril Spiers; and Bill Jones.
2 Fred Stansfield, Alf Sherwood and Danny Malloy.
3 Stan Richards, Wilf Grant and Derek Tapscott.
4 Arsenal; the attendance was 57,893 and the score was 0–0. Despite dropping a point (and another 2 when we beat them at Highbury a few weeks earlier), the Gunners went on to win the title that year.
5 City won 4–1 at Old Trafford, then beat Liverpool 4–0 at Ninian two days later. And Manchester City? We beat them 6–0. Obviously!
6 Wolves, and Gerry Hitchens. Wolves were runners-up that season.
7 We lost 9–1. Our goal was a late consolation from Ron Stockin, who had previously played for Wolves. The visitors were 5–0 up at half-time. As they jogged towards the tunnel, a City grandstander shouted to Wolves skipper Billy Wright, 'You haven't won this yet, Billy!' Billy looked up and replied, 'No, but we've got a bloody good chance…!'
8 Trevor Ford; Gerry Hitchens again; and Mike Tiddy.
9 Sunderland, Kidderminster Harriers and Torquay United.
10 Derek Tapscott, who then joined us from the Gunners five years later; and Worcester City.
11 The goalie was Ken Jones; the forward was Ron Hewitt.

1 Greg Farrell.
2 Georgie Johnston.
3 Jimmy McInch.
4 Nigel Rees.
5 Peter Sayer.
6 Tony Villars.
7 Jason Gummer.
8 Chris Fry.
9 Lee Jarman.
10 Simon Haworth.
11 Nathan Cadette.

1 Club founder Bartley Wilson.
2 Andy Jordan.
3 Christian Roberts.
4 Jason Fowler.
5 Phil Bater and Phil Kite.
6 Jim Eadie and Jason Perry.
7 Mark Aizlewood.
8 Paul Wimbleton.
9 Russell Osman.
10 Dai Ward and Ron Nicholls (who returned to Bristol to join Bristol City).
11 Johnny Watkins and Peter Hooper.

Between the Wars

1 Both played for Cardiff: they were Fred Keenor (Wales) and Jimmy Blair (Scotland). And both, according to the custom of the time, sported their City socks.

2 City finished level with Huddersfield on 57 points. Huddersfield won the title on goal average, by 0.024 of a goal. Goal average – which was 'goals scored' divided by 'goals conceded' - was replaced in the Football League in 1976 by the much simpler and more logical calculation called goal difference – which is 'goals scored' minus 'goals conceded'. In 1924, had goal difference been used, both teams would have had 'plus 27'. But Huddersfield, with 60 scored and 33 conceded, had scored one less than City's total of 61 scored and 34 conceded – so City would have won the title on 'goals scored'. In any event, it was the closest-ever League title race up to that point, and has only been rivalled since then by the Arsenal-Liverpool nerve-tingler of 1989.

3 Len Davies – who actually scored more League goals in his City career (129) than anyone else. Alas, on this occasion his spot kick was saved by Birmingham keeper Dan Tremelling, who went on to be capped by England.

4 Harry Wake.

5 Willie Davies was confined to his hospital bed in Talgarth, due to pleurisy, for several months in 1926–27. His replacement, Billy Thirlaway, was signed from Birmingham in March 1927 – unfortunately after he had already appeared

for the Brummies in that season's FA Cup. Inside forward
Ernie Curtis ended up playing at outside-right in the final.

6   They had conceded fewer goals than anyone else in the
    division. Unfortunately, they had also scored the fewest.

7   Ernie Curtis. City finished bottom of Division Three South,
    and – only seven years after winning the Cup – had to apply
    for re-election. Luckily, they were successfully re-elected by
    the 92 League clubs, and so retained their League status.

8   Jimmy McCambridge. He won 4 caps for Ireland, 2 of them
    earned whilst he was at City.

9   Another Jim – Jimmy Collins.

10 Reggie Pugh, from Aberaman. Unfortunately, Reggie was
    one of those players who lost most of his career due to an
    unfortunate event called the Second World War.

11 Billy Baker, who recovered successfully from having been a
    'guest' of the Japanese during the war.

Bibliography

This book is all our own work. We know our stuff.

Or at least we think we do.

Just to be sure though, we have occasionally consulted other historical sources to corroborate information, check dates and spellings or even just settle arguments between ourselves.

The following are examples of books and publications which we as authors have found to be reliable. Once again, we happily recommend these works to any fan of Cardiff City FC, 'The greatest team in football, the world has ever seen...'

Clark, Brian & Shepherd, Richard, *Real, Robins & Bluebirds: The Autobiography of 'Goal Scorer' Brian Clark* (Skipton: Vertical Editions, 2006)

Collins, David, *Born Under a Grange End Star* (Sigma, 2002)

Collins, David and Bennett, Gareth, *Never Mind the Bluebirds: The Ultimate Cardiff City Quiz Book* (Stroud: The History Press, 2012)

Crooks, John, *Cardiff City Chronology, 1920–86* (Pontypool: self-published, 1986)

Crooks, John, *The Bluebirds: A Who's Who of Cardiff City League Players* (Pontypool: self-published, 1987)

Hayes, Dean, *Cardiff City Football Club: An A-Z* (Cardiff: Aureus, 1998)

Hayes, Dean, *The South Wales Derbies: A History of Cardiff City versus Swansea City* (The Parrs Wood Press, 2003)

Hayes, Dean, *The Who's Who of Cardiff City* (Breedon Books, 2006)

Jackson, Peter, *The Cardiff City Story* (Cardiff: S.A. Brain & Co, 1974)

Jenkins, Derrick, and Stennet, Ceri, *Wembley 1927: The Cardiff-Arsenal FA Cup Final 1927* (Cardiff: self-published, 1989)